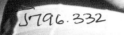

CREATIVE EDUCATION

**TAMPA BAY
BUCCANEERS**

JULIE NELSON

Published by Creative Education
123 South Broad Street, Mankato, Minnesota 56001
Creative Education is an imprint of The Creative Company

Designed by Rita Marshall

Photos by: Allsport USA, SportsChrome

Library of Congress Cataloging-in-Publication Data

Nelson, Julie.
Tampa Bay Buccaneers / by Julie Nelson.
p. cm. — (NFL today)
Summary: Traces the history of the Tampa Bay Buccaneers from its beginnings
through 1999.
ISBN 1-58341-061-9

1. Tampa Bay Buccaneers (Football team)—History—Juvenile literature.
[1. Tampa Bay Buccaneers (Football team)—History. 2. Football—History.]
I. Title. II. Series: NFL today (Mankato, Minn.)

GV956.T35N45   2000
796.332'64'0975965—dc21   99-023744

First edition

9 8 7 6 5 4 3 2 1

The western part of Florida along the Gulf of Mexico is called "the Suncoast." It is an area blessed with warm sunshine and bright economic growth. Much of that growth is concentrated around Tampa Bay, one of the busiest harbors in the United States. Tampa Bay is flanked by two major cities—Tampa on the east side and St. Petersburg on the west.

The Tampa Bay area has a long and interesting history. The Spaniard Ponce de Leon explored the region in his search for the legendary Fountain of Youth in the early 1500s. More than three centuries later, Cuban immigrants, at-

First-round draft pick Lee Roy Selmon led Tampa Bay as a rookie with five sacks.

tracted by Tampa's Spanish heritage, established a thriving cigar industry there. Such an industry was only fitting, since the name "Tampa" means "sticks of fire."

The National Football League took notice of the rising population around Tampa Bay in the mid-1900s. In 1974, the NFL granted an expansion franchise to the region to begin playing in 1976. The team, based in Tampa, would be called the Tampa Bay Buccaneers, making it the only franchise in the NFL to be named after a body of water rather than a city or state.

The "Bucs" have struggled at or near the bottom of the league for much of their history, setting several records in futility. Still, their fans have remained loyal and hopeful, and it appears that their optimism may soon be rewarded. The Buccaneers, tired of walking the plank for so many years, may soon be pillaging the league instead.

STUMBLING AT THE START

Optimism was high in Tampa Bay for the Buccaneers' first season. Team owner Hugh Culverhouse, an attorney who purchased the franchise for $16 million, hired a head coach who knew a lot about winning—John McKay from the University of Southern California. McKay's USC teams had won nine conference titles, five Rose Bowls, and four national championships in the 1960s and '70s. In Tampa, however, McKay would soon learn a lot about losing.

McKay, realizing that success would not come overnight, told reporters that he had a five-year plan to make the Bucs great. Why five years? "It's simple," he said. "I had a five-year

The 1999 Defensive Player of the Year, Warren Sapp.

1 9 7 7

In his first NFL season, running back Ricky Bell led the Bucs in rushing with 436 yards.

contract. If I would have had a six-year contract, I would have had a six-year plan."

McKay probably felt like revising his timeline once the club actually began playing. In 1976, Tampa Bay became the only team in modern NFL history to lose every game in a season, going 0–14. Things were so bad that the team's first starting quarterback, Steve Spurrier, was released as soon as the 1976 season ended.

The addition of three new quarterbacks and an outstanding runner—number one draft pick Ricky Bell from USC—did little to improve the Bucs' offense in 1977. The Bucs scored only 53 points while losing their first 12 games. That made the club's all-time record 0–26. In game 13 against the New Orleans Saints, the Buccaneers defenders decided to take over the job of scoring themselves. They ran three interceptions back for touchdowns to earn a 33–17 victory and halt the losing streak.

More than 74,000 fans packed Tampa Stadium to see the Bucs win their first home game, 17–7, in the season finale against St. Louis. It seemed that Coach McKay's five-year plan was finally showing signs of working.

THE FIRST GREAT BUCCANEERS

It was clear from the start that the Buccaneers' defense was the heart of the team, and that the heart of that unit was defensive end Lee Roy Selmon, the first player McKay had drafted in 1976. McKay had been impressed by the All-American's play at the University of Oklahoma, where he helped the Sooners win the 1975 national championship.

8

At 6-foot-3 and 255 pounds, Selmon was average-sized for an NFL defensive lineman, but his talent was anything but average. "During the game, Lee Roy never says a word," said Chicago Bears offensive lineman Ted Albrecht. "He just lines up on every play and then comes whirling in like a tornado. I've been told that if you get him mad, he's almost impossible to block. I'm glad I've never gotten him mad."

In Tampa Bay's first win against New Orleans in 1977, Selmon had led the defensive effort, making 12 tackles and three sacks. His constant pressure on Saints quarterback Archie Manning also had been largely responsible for the Bucs' three interceptions.

Selmon continued to star for the Buccaneers until his retirement after the 1984 season. He stayed in the community, however, and helped to develop a strong athletic program at Tampa's University of South Florida. The entire Tampa Bay area celebrated in 1995 when Selmon became the first Buccaneers player elected to the Pro Football Hall of Fame.

Although Lee Roy Selmon sparked a respectable Tampa Bay defense, the offense still lacked a leader. John McKay believed he finally had the right man for the job when he drafted quarterback Doug Williams from Grambling in 1978. At 6-foot-4 and 215 pounds, Williams had the size and strength (he could throw a ball 80 yards in the air) to do the job, but—the experts pointed out—historically, few black quarterbacks had done well in the NFL.

Williams proudly challenged his critics. "Race has nothing to do with what I can and cannot do," he said with determination. "I feel I'm a solid pro quarterback who will get better with experience. And whether I'm green, black, purple, or

1 9 7 8

Coach John McKay led the Buccaneers to their best record yet at 5–11.

Offensive tackle Paul Gruber.

All-Pro linebacker Hardy Nickerson.   11

1 9 7 9

Tight end Jimmie Giles emerged as a star, leading Tampa Bay with seven touchdowns.

yellow, the only thing that counts is my performance out on the field."

Williams then went out and backed up his words. In 1978, the Tampa Bay offense, featuring Williams, Ricky Bell, and newly acquired receiver Jimmie Giles, helped the team post a much-improved 5–11 record. The Bucs defense—anchored by linebackers Richard Wood and Dewey Selmon—also showed signs of greatness, allowing more than 19 points only three times all season. It would only get better for Tampa fans the following year.

The Bucs won their opening game in 1979 and then kept on winning. With one week left in the season, the team's record stood at 9–6. A victory in its last game at home against Kansas City would give Tampa Bay the NFC Central Division crown and a berth in the playoffs. Playing in a heavy downpour on a muddy field, the Buccaneers' defense was magnificent. The only points of the 3–0 victory came on a field goal by Bucs kicker Neil O'Donoghue. Ecstatic fans in Tampa Stadium proudly held up banners that read: "From Worst to First."

There were some other firsts that year, too. Ricky Bell became Tampa Bay's first 1,000-yard rusher, finishing the year with 1,263 yards on the ground. In addition, Lee Roy Selmon became the Bucs' first award winner when he was named the NFC's Defensive Player of the Year. McKay's five-year plan had taken only four years, and Doug Williams—in only his second year in the league—had led his team to the playoffs for the first time in its history.

In the first round of the playoffs, the Bucs faced the Philadelphia Eagles. McKay decided to use mainly a ground attack, and Bell responded with 142 yards rushing and two touchdowns to lead the Bucs to a 24–17 win. Tampa Bay then went into the NFC championship game to play the Los Angeles Rams at Tampa Stadium. A win would mean a trip to the Super Bowl.

The game turned out to be a defensive struggle, with neither team scoring a touchdown all afternoon. Every time the Rams approached the Tampa Bay goal line, Lee Roy Selmon, lineman Randy Crowder, linebacker Richard Wood, and the rest of the Bucs defenders found a way to stop them. Unfortunately, the Tampa Bay offense was just as ineffective against the Rams' defense, and Los Angeles won 9–0. Bucs fans were disappointed but not depressed. They finally had a winner.

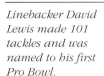

Linebacker David Lewis made 101 tackles and was named to his first Pro Bowl.

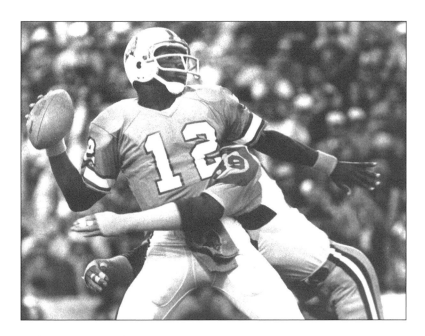

Doug Williams was Tampa Bay's first quarterback star.

13

1 9 8 0

Linebacker Dewey Selmon (#61) teamed up with his brother, defensive end Lee Roy Selmon.

The Bucs fell to earth in 1980, finishing 5–10–1. Still, Doug Williams continued to improve, throwing for almost 3,400 yards. The club also added an outstanding young receiver, Kevin House, who quickly became one of Williams's favorite targets. The next year, McKay acquired some more young talent in the NFL draft, taking All-American linebacker Hugh Green in the first round and running back James Wilder in the second.

Strengthened on both defense and offense, the Buccaneers bounced back with a 9–7 record, another division title, and a playoff berth in 1981. Unfortunately, the Bucs were quickly eliminated by the Dallas Cowboys in a 38–0 first-round rout. Tampa Bay reached the playoffs again in 1982, but another loss to Dallas, this time by a 30–17 margin, ended the Bucs' championship hopes. Tampa Bay fans didn't know it yet, but it would be a long time before their club would be a winner again.

The 1983 season marked a turning point for the Buccaneers franchise. Tampa Bay's offense suffered a devastating blow when Doug Williams departed to join a club in the new United States Football League. Without an experienced quarterback, the Bucs started the season 0–9 and finished with a dismal 2–14 record.

There was one bright spot for the team, however. Coach McKay decided to concentrate on building a rushing attack around third-year halfback James Wilder, who was now more than ready for the opportunity. Wilder was a big and tireless runner who wanted the ball on every play. "When

Steve DeBerg succeeded Williams as the Bucs' quarterback.

James Wilder was a fiery runner.

my number is called," he explained, "it's my turn to make things happen."

Wilder led the team in rushing in 1983, despite playing much of the season with broken ribs. In one game, he set a club record with 219 yards on the ground. Wilder finished the year with 1,544 yards rushing, but he led the Bucs in receiving as well, pulling in 85 catches for 685 yards. The next year, he set an NFL record with 407 carries in a season, a mark that would stand for 14 years. In short, Wilder was practically the entire Tampa Bay offense.

Unfortunately, Wilder's record-setting year in 1984 was offset by the team's disappointing 6–10 record. Head coach John McKay decided to retire. McKay's replacement, Leeman Bennett, believed the club was close to turning things around again. "I expect our team to contend for the NFC Central Division title now, not later," he said at the start of the 1985 season.

Despite Coach Bennett's confidence, success was not within Tampa Bay's reach. The team finished at 2–14 in both 1985 and 1986, falling to the bottom of the NFL standings. 1986 marked the fourth straight year of 10 or more defeats, and Bennett was fired.

But there was even more heartbreaking news. Tampa Bay had selected first in the 1986 NFL draft and was counting on its top pick—Heisman Trophy-winning running back Bo Jackson from Auburn—to be the team's future star. Jackson decided to play baseball for the Kansas City Royals instead, however, and never played a single down for the Buccaneers. In addition, the Bucs had made a trade with the San Francisco 49ers in 1986, dealing away backup quarterback

1 9 8 4

Linebacker Jeff Davis led the team in tackles (165) for the first of three straight seasons.

The Bucs' rushing attack was one of the NFL's best (pages 18-19).   17

Steve Young, who would later emerge as one of the finest signal-callers in the NFL.

With their poor record in 1986, the Bucs earned the right to pick first in the 1987 draft as well. This time, new coach Ray Perkins made sure to select someone who wanted to play a part in Tampa's revival.

1 9 8 7

Rookie Vinny Testaverde threw for 1,081 yards and five touchdowns as a backup.

TESTAVERDE HITS TAMPA

The Bucs didn't have to look far for their new star, quarterback Vinny Testaverde. He was playing college ball at the University of Miami, a few hundred miles south, where he won the Heisman Trophy in 1986.

Testaverde had great arm strength and accuracy. In two seasons at the helm, he led Miami to a 21–3 record. Many fans, however, chose to focus on the few games Testaverde had lost rather than on all of the games he had won. Two of those losses had come in bowl games in which Testaverde played poorly. Whether fair or not, he had earned a reputation for choking in big games.

Nevertheless, Perkins made Testaverde his number one pick. Later in the draft, the Bucs coach selected a terrific young receiver, Mark Carrier from Nicholls State in Louisiana, to complement his new quarterback.

Testaverde quickly impressed the Bucs coaches with both his ability and his attitude. He worked long hours to prepare himself for the fast pace of the NFL. As the 1987 season began, Testaverde waited on the bench while veteran Steve DeBerg ran the team, but he would soon get his chance. The Bucs, who had gotten off to a hot start, went into a tailspin in the second half of the season. Suddenly, Perkins turned to Testaverde to try to halt the losing streak. Tampa Bay lost all four of Testaverde's starts to finish at 4–11, but the young quarterback showed promise, throwing for more than 1,000 yards in the four contests. By the start of the 1988 season, Testaverde had been designated as the team's offensive leader.

Testaverde struggled in his early years in Tampa Bay, particularly when it came to keeping his passes out of the hands of defenders. Perkins showed patience with his new quarterback, but the fans didn't. Boos resounded in Tampa Stadium as the Bucs continued to lose regularly. "It's not fun to be me as a football player right now," Testaverde admitted. "What would really please me is to go out and play great. That would shut everybody up."

Second-year wide-out Mark Carrier, the team's top deep threat, posted 970 receiving yards.

Steve Young quarterbacked the Bucs for just one season.

Star passer Vinny Testaverde.

Refusing to let himself get discouraged, Testaverde slowly began to improve his passing accuracy and began connecting regularly with Mark Carrier and Bruce Hill for big gains. Yet the club still had trouble winning. By the early 1990s, Perkins was gone, and Testaverde would soon follow.

When new coach Sam Wyche arrived in Tampa Bay in 1992, he immediately made some dramatic changes. Wyche began emphasizing running over passing, and halfback Reggie Cobb responded by gaining more than 1,100 yards. Coach Wyche also drafted quarterback Craig Erickson out of Miami and began grooming him to succeed Testaverde, who was released before the next season and signed with the Cleveland Browns.

1 9 9 2

Reggie Cobb was the first Bucs rusher in seven years to run for more than 1,000 yards.

SHAKING THINGS UP IN THE '90S

In letting Testaverde go, Coach Wyche seemed to be saying, "We're making a clean break with the past and looking only toward the future." The changes began in 1993, with Erickson taking over at quarterback, rookie lineman Eric Curry adding to the pass rush, and All-Pro linebacker Hardy Nickerson signing on as a free agent to add his special brand of aggressiveness to the defense.

Wyche continued to shake things up in 1994, especially on offense. Even though he already had Erickson, Wyche could not resist taking Fresno State All-American quarterback Trent Dilfer with the sixth pick in the 1994 NFL draft. Wyche soon decided to start Dilfer ahead of Erickson.

In the second round of the draft, Wyche selected running back Errict Rhett from the University of Florida. Rhett immediately became the starting halfback when Reggie Cobb left to sign with the Green Bay Packers. The rookie became the fourth 1,000-yard rusher in Bucs history in 1994 and then surpassed that milestone in his second year as well.

1 9 9 5

In his first full season as a starter, Trent Dilfer passed for 2,774 yards.

Despite Rhett's success, the team continued to struggle in 1995. Receiver Alvin Harper—a new acquisition—was hurt for part of the season, and Dilfer suffered through a terrible second-season slump, throwing 18 interceptions and only four touchdown passes. After getting off to a fast 5–2 start, the Bucs faded back in the standings, finishing at 7–9. That was the team's best record since 1982, but it wasn't good enough for Tampa Bay's fans or owners. Sam Wyche was sent packing. Named as his replacement was Tony Dungy, former defensive coordinator for the Minnesota Vikings.

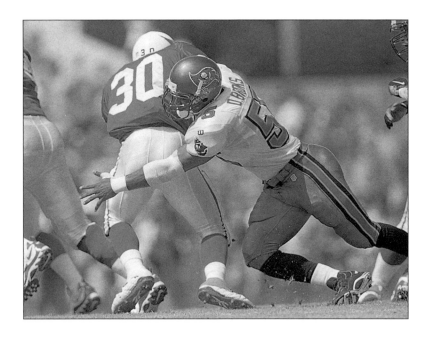

Fast and ferocious linebacker Derrick Brooks.

Dungy, who played defensive back for the Super Bowl champion Pittsburgh Steelers in the 1970s, had long established himself as one of the most innovative defensive coaches in the NFL. He had been a finalist for a number of head coaching positions and was delighted to land the Bucs job. "I see myself coming into a positive situation," Dungy explained. "People have a right to expect this team to become a winner."

Fans would have to continue to wait, though, at least through 1996. After losing their first five games, the Bucs went on to finish the season 6–10. Tampa fans had hoped for a better record, but Dungy's vision for the future had begun to take shape, particularly with an aggressive defense that had earned respect throughout the league.

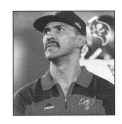

1 9 9 7

Second-year head coach Tony Dungy led the Bucs back to respectability with a 10–6 record.

THE NEW-LOOK BUCS

The Tampa Bay offense was given a boost in 1996 with the second-round draft selection of Mike Alstott, a bruising 6-foot-1 and 248-pound fullback out of Purdue University. College legends had it that he trained by pushing his jeep across parking lots and running with tires strapped to his body. "I never wanted to be a fireman or a doctor," Alstott explained. "The only thing I ever wanted to do was be an NFL player."

Alstott was a powerful yet agile runner who could do it all—run, block, and catch passes. In his first season, he led the Bucs with six touchdowns and set a new Bucs rookie record by catching 65 passes. With Alstott added to Tampa Bay's young but aggressive lineup, the Buccaneers appeared ready to plunder the NFL in 1997.

The NFL's most versatile fullback, Mike Alstott (pages 26-27).

The Bucs were armed with a new logo and new red, black, and pewter uniforms, but they seemed to have a new attitude as well. They began the 1997 season by stunning San Francisco 13–6. The win was due in large part to the inspired play of one of Tampa Bay's most promising defensive players: tackle Warren Sapp.

Sapp had been a potential top five draft pick in 1995. After reports of failed drug tests surfaced, however, he dropped to the 12th selection in the draft. Though Sapp admitted to making mistakes in the past, he was determined to overcome them and promised to repay Tampa Bay for its trust. "The Bucs won't be 26th or 27th in the league in defensive stats anymore," he said confidently. "With me here, there'll be no more numbers like that."

Hard-hitting safety John Lynch earned a Pro Bowl berth with 107 tackles.

Ball-hawking cornerback Donnie Abraham.

Sapp made good on that promise in 1997, finishing the year with 10.5 sacks and establishing himself as one of the league's top tackles. Not coincidentally, Tampa Bay's defense leapfrogged to third in the league as Sapp, linebackers Hardy Nickerson and Derrick Brooks, and linemen Brad Culpepper and Chidi Ahanotu joined forces to record a team-record 44 sacks.

Linebacker Derrick Brooks led Tampa Bay's defense with 153 tackles.

Tampa Bay's defense wasn't the only game in town, though. The team's offense was improved as well, due mainly to a fierce and unrelenting ground attack driven by Alstott and tailback Warrick Dunn, a new arrival. Dunn, who would be named the NFL Offensive Rookie of the Year, set a new Tampa Bay rookie record for total yards with 1,440. Together, the powerful Alstott and ultra-quick Dunn became known as "Thunder and Lightning."

The Bucs surprised the league in 1997 by finishing 10–6 and qualifying for the playoffs for the first time in 15 years. They surprised even more people in the first round, holding off Barry Sanders's Detroit Lions for a 20–10 win. The Bucs' dream season, however, was finally brought to an end the next week by defending Super Bowl champion Green Bay.

SAILING FOR SUCCESS

Buccaneers team owner and president Malcolm Glazer was pleased with the team's 1997 results. In only his second season, Coach Dungy had led the Bucs to their best finish since 1979. Glazer took steps to make winning a permanent habit by extending Dungy's contract into the 2002 season. "When my family took ownership of this team in

Electrifying tailback Warrick Dunn.

Explosive defensive end Chidi Ahanotu.   31

The Buccaneers expected wideout Keyshawn Johnson to make big offensive contributions.

1995, we pledged to bring a championship to Tampa Bay," Glazer explained. "We have no doubt that Tony will be the person to one day bring a title to our loyal fans."

Although the Bucs missed the playoffs in 1998, they rebounded with a breakthrough season in 1999. Behind one of the league's toughest defenses, the Buccaneers went 11–5 and captured their first NFC Central Division title in 18 years.

After a first-round playoff bye, the Bucs took on the Washington Redskins under the leadership of a rookie quarterback. Shaun King had been promoted to the starting role after Dilfer suffered a season-ending injury, and he quickly proved he was no typical rookie. King, nicknamed "Smoothie" by teammates due to his poise under pressure, guided the Bucs past the Redskins, overcoming a 13-point halftime deficit. Although Tampa Bay lost 11–6 to St. Louis the next week, the Buccaneers were clearly a team on the rise.

After the season, the Bucs made it clear that Shaun King was their quarterback of the future by releasing Dilfer. They also dramatically improved their offense by trading for All-Pro receiver Keyshawn Johnson. With these young stars added to the Buccaneers' already loaded roster, a Super Bowl trophy may very soon be docking in Tampa Bay.